MAR 1 8

# MONSTER FISH!

## True Stories of Adventures With Animals

**Zeb Hogan**
**With Kathleen Weidner Zoehfeld**

## NATIONAL GEOGRAPHIC

WASHINGTON, D.C.

Since 1888, the National Geographic Society has
funded more than 12,000 research, exploration, and
preservation projects around the world. The Society
receives funds from National Geographic Partners,
LLC, funded in part by your purchase. A portion of
the proceeds from this book supports this vital work.
To learn more, visit natgeo.com/info.

NATIONAL GEOGRAPHIC and Yellow Border
Design are trademarks of the National Geographic
Society, used under license.

For more information, visit nationalgeographic.com,
call 1-800-647-5463, or write to the following address:

National Geographic Partners
1145 17th Street N.W.
Washington, D.C. 20036-4688 U.S.A.

Visit us online at nationalgeographic.com/books

For librarians and teachers: ngchildrensbooks.org

More for kids from National Geographic:
kids.nationalgeographic.com

For information about special discounts for bulk
purchases, please contact National Geographic Books
Special Sales: specialsales@natgeo.com

For rights or permissions inquiries, please contact
National Geographic Books Subsidiary Rights:
bookrights@natgeo.com

Art directed by Sanjida Rashid
Designed by Ruth Ann Thompson

National Geographic supports K–12
educators with ELA Common Core
Resources. Visit natgeoed.org/
commoncore for more information.

Trade paperback ISBN: 978-1-4263-2703-2
Reinforced library edition ISBN: 978-1-4263-2704-9

Printed in China
16/RRDS/1

# Table of CONTENTS

**MONSTER OF THE MEKONG**     6

    Chapter 1: A Rare Giant     8

    Chapter 2: Megafish Madness     16

    Chapter 3: A Big Catch     26

**FISH SUPERPOWERS**     36

    Chapter 1: Super Biters     38

    Chapter 2: Super Shockers     48

    Chapter 3: Super Swimmers     58

**IN SEARCH OF GIANT STINGRAYS**     70

    Chapter 1: Biggest in the World?     72

    Chapter 2: Hide-and-Seek     82

    Chapter 3: Protecting Giants     92

**DON'T MISS!**     101

Index and More Information     110

# Monster Fish MAP

NORTH AMERICA

EUROPE

PACIFIC OCEAN

ATLANTIC OCEAN

### Fish ranges

- American paddlefish
- Chinook salmon
- Chinook salmon ocean range
- Electric eel
- Giant freshwater stingray
- Mekong giant catfish
- New Zealand longfin eel
- Payara
- Piraiba
- Piranha
- Wolffish

SOUTH AMERICA

ASIA

AFRICA

PACIFIC
OCEAN

INDIAN
OCEAN

AUSTRALIA

ANTARCTICA

These are some of the fish
we talk about in this book.
Here's where they live!

# MONSTER of the MEKONG

It takes five people to hold this captured Mekong catfish.

Local fishermen use a tarp to lift a giant catfish out of the river.

# Chapter 1

# A RARE GIANT

There's a little village that sits on the banks of the Mekong (sounds like MEE-kong) River in northern Thailand. Every year, the villagers eagerly await the arrival of the rainy season. It begins in early May. As the rain falls, the river rises. Many types of fish begin to swim upriver to lay their eggs. The villagers are looking to catch a very special kind of fish.

Early each morning, local fishers climb into their long, narrow boats and slip quietly into the river. One boat holds three or four fishermen. And each boat has its *mong lai,* or fishing net, ready. These nets are made from thick twine. They are made to catch giants!

The fishers paddle to a well-known spot on the river. It's a place where their parents and grandparents fished before them. The Mekong is a long, winding river with plenty of rocks and rapids that could tangle and tear nets. But in this area, the river runs straight and shallow.

The fishers take turns setting out their nets. One long edge of each net stays afloat. The rest of the net slowly sinks down. It spreads out under the muddy water.

Then the fishermen wait. With a little luck, they will soon have fish in their nets. For hundreds of years, fish from this river have been an important source of food for the local people.

The river is home to many types of fish. The redtail catfish gets its name from its brightly colored tail. The beady-eyed goonch has long, fleshy whiskers and spotted skin. The small carp, *pla soi,* is a special favorite. Fishers catch them by the thousands. Cooks mix the fish with salt and rice bran in large clay pots. They let the mixture sit for weeks, or even months. People say the longer the fish ferments in the pot, the better it tastes! But of all the fish, there is one more important than the rest: the Mekong giant catfish.

Here in the village of Hat Khrai, (sounds like hot KRY) this fish is revered. The street signs have giant catfish on them. The village has a giant catfish museum, complete with a 50-foot (15-m)-long giant catfish statue. And people wear T-shirts that say "Hat Khrai: Home of the World's Largest Freshwater Fish!"

In the Thai language, the giant catfish is called *pla buek*, or "big fish." Legends say giant catfish as big as 770 pounds (350 kg) and 10 feet (3 m) long have been found in the river. But that was a long time ago.

In years past, when the fishing was good, a dozen or more boats would line up, waiting for a chance to catch a giant catfish. One morning in May 2005, a group of young fishermen decided to borrow a net and try.

**Did You Know?**

The Mekong giant catfish is a gentle giant. It has no teeth and feeds mainly on the algae and other soft plants growing on the rocks in the riverbed.

But no one expected to catch a giant.

These young fishermen had grown up watching their fathers and grandfathers net giant catfish from the river. But in the past three years, not a single wild giant catfish had been caught anywhere along the Mekong in Thailand. Were any giant catfish left? That morning the fishermen were in for a big surprise.

They had only been fishing for a short time when they heard a splash. They saw a wide, silvery tail rise up out of the water. It whacked the surface. A big fish was tangled in their net! It took them more than an hour to haul the struggling giant to shore. Eight men lifted the fish out of the water.

Because giant catfish have become so rare, biologists (sounds like bye-OL-uh-jists) from the Thai Department of Fisheries stay in Hat Khrai during the catfish-fishing season.

If a female catfish is caught, the biologists gather the fish's eggs. Later, they can use the eggs to breed baby giant catfish in captivity.

The biologists soon heard about the important catch. The fish was almost nine feet (2.7 m) long, and it weighed 646 pounds (293 kg). The fishers did not know it yet, but they had just caught the biggest freshwater fish in the world.

The fish was a female. The biologists gathered her eggs. But before she could be released back into the river, she died. Her death was a loss to the river and to science.

# The Mekong River

The Mekong River is one of the world's largest rivers. It runs more than 2,700 miles (4,350 km). It spans six countries: China, Myanmar, Laos, Thailand, Cambodia, and Vietnam. The Mekong River supports the largest inland fishery in the world. Of the 60 million people who live in the lower Mekong Basin, 80 percent rely on the river system for their food and livelihoods. This area is one of the richest areas of biodiversity (sounds like BYE-oh-duh-VUR-si-tee) in the world.

Zeb Hogan wants to meet monsters—monster fish, that is!

# MEGAFISH MADNESS

**M**y name is Zeb Hogan, and I am a freshwater fish biologist. When scientists talk about "freshwater fish," they usually mean any type of fish that spends most of its life in a lake or river rather than in the salty water of the ocean. I study the largest types of these fish. Word of that record-breaking Mekong giant catfish didn't take long to reach me.

I'll admit I was curious. By the time the fish was caught, I had been doing research on the Mekong for several years. I was studying the many types of fish that move, or migrate, up the river to lay their eggs.

I spent a lot of time in Thailand, Laos, and Cambodia, traveling up and down the river. I talked with fishers, visited local fish markets, and tried to learn everything I could about the local fish.

As soon as I heard the news of the giant catfish, I hurried to Hat Khrai to learn more about it. It certainly was a monster! But during my time on the river, people had told me stories of even bigger fish. Different kinds of fish—carp, goonch, stingrays— fish that were more than 16 feet (4.9 m) long and weighed more than 1,000 pounds

(454 kg)! As I stared at the photos of the newly caught giant, a question entered my mind: *Is the Mekong giant catfish really the world's largest freshwater fish?*

We know that the African elephant is the world's largest land animal. The blue whale is the biggest animal in the ocean, and the whale shark is the world's largest saltwater fish. But what is the largest freshwater fish? I started doing some research. It was soon clear to me that no one really knew! I also realized that if I wanted the answer, I was going to have to find it myself. But it wasn't going to be easy. I would need some help. The National Geographic Society supports the work of many scientists and explorers around the world. I explained my question

to them, and they were interested, too!
I soon became a National Geographic
Explorer, and my quest to find, study, and
protect the world's largest fish had begun.

Across the world, there are about
30 different types, or species (sounds like
SPEE-sheez), of freshwater fish that grow
to enormous size. I call them megafish.

A megafish is any species that can grow
to more than six feet (1.8 m) long or weigh
more than 200 pounds (91 kg). Each of
these megafish species is very different
from the others, and nobody knows very
much about them. They live beneath the
surface of the world's great rivers and
lakes. They are rare and elusive creatures—
sort of like the Loch Ness Monster!
Except that these creatures are not

made-up, mythological monsters. They are 100 percent real! But megafish, despite their monster size, are still a mega mystery.

The Mekong River is home to more types of megafish than any other river in the world. And in my time on the river, I've seen some really awesome fish. The most impressive thing about megafish is, of course, their size. Any fish larger than me is a big fish!

And their rarity makes them even more special. I first saw a giant catfish back in 1997, when a friend of mine invited me up to Hat Khrai during catfish-fishing season.

# Growing Awareness

People are starting to become more aware of the Mekong giant catfish. When I began my quest, I would show people photos of different types of giant fish. Even people who had lived all their lives near the river did not recognize them! Now when I speak to students, many of them can name these fish.

While I was there, fishers caught one. It was about seven feet (2.1 m) long and weighed 400 pounds (181 kg). For the first time, I got a close-up look at a giant catfish. It had large eyes and an unusual, down-turned mouth. Its skin felt like wet rubber.

I sensed how powerful it must be when it is at home in the river. But after being caught, it was exhausted, helpless, and hurt. I'll never forget that moment. I had assumed, like most people, that rivers and lakes were home to smaller fish and the ocean was home to larger fish. The idea that a giant like this one could live in a river changed the way I thought about freshwater. This giant was proof that there was still so much to be learned about the mysterious creatures that live there.

It made me determined to learn more.
It also made me want to protect them.

Over the years, biologists have seen
that adult giant catfish live in the deepest
parts of the Mekong for much of the
dry season. In fact, deep pools all along
the Mekong are named after these
massive fish. During the rainy season,
they gather together. Then they swim
hundreds of kilometers upstream to lay
their eggs, or spawn.

We know that much, but not much
more. The Mekong giant catfish might
be famous, but they are not well studied,
especially in the wild.

For example, we don't know exactly
how far they migrate, or where exactly
they spawn, or how long they live, or

even why they
are disappearing.
We need this
basic information
in order to protect
the species. So, it's a
race against the clock to
learn more about the giant
catfish before they disappear forever.

I was very sad that the record-breaking
catfish of Hat Khrai had died. If only I'd
had a chance to tag the fish and release
it back into the river alive. I could have
had a chance to learn more about these
fish. From that point on, I was determined
to find, catch, and tag a few of these
magnificent monsters. Little did I know
how long it would take!

Villagers in Cambodia come out to see this captured Mekong giant catfish.

# A BIG CATCH

The Mekong is an ancient river that began flowing long before there were any humans on Earth. The river has many natural habitats—from fast-flowing rapids to deep, quiet pools. During the rainy season, the river's vast flood plains provide fish with many sources of food. Many fish have evolved to have long life spans and grow to extraordinary size.

But so much has changed on the river. Even in the past 20 years! Today, more than 60 million people from six different countries live close to the Mekong.

Most of those people depend on the river for fish. This has put a strain on things. So many fish are taken out so quickly, the fish don't have a chance to breed and replace their numbers.

People use the river in other ways, too. Some stretches of the river, and many of its branches, or tributaries (sounds like TRIB-yuh-ter-ees), have fast-flowing currents. The energy of these currents can be captured to provide people with electrical power.

Many hydroelectric dams have been built on tributaries of the Mekong. In some areas, government officials are thinking

about damming
the main stream
of the Mekong as well.
But a dam on the main
stream would keep fish from
reaching their spawning grounds.

If fish are not allowed to spawn, there
will be no young to replace the older
fish when they die. Not just the giant
catfish, but many migrating species would
also be in danger of dying out completely.
Dams, overfishing, pollution, and
shrinking habitats have taken a harsh
toll on all the river's fish. But its giants
are the ones hit hardest.

For many years now, it's been my
mission on the Mekong to tag a giant
catfish, to follow its spawning migration.

Tagging allows biologists to identify individual fish, track their movements, and estimate how many of them there are in any particular area. Fish are different from animals that live on land. Land animals are easier to see, follow, and count. Fish live underwater, so we use tags to keep track of them even when we can't see them. If we tag a fish in Cambodia and it's caught later in Thailand, we know the fish moved from Cambodia to Thailand. If we catch a fish and it's longer than when we tagged it last year, we can calculate the fish's growth rate.

But tagging a wild giant catfish isn't easy. I made friends with the people of Hat Khrai. I put together a team of expert fishers to help me. We needed boats and other equipment. And I had to get permission from the Thai government to do the tagging. The hardest part, however, was finding a fish to tag!

Mekong giant catfish are "critically endangered." This means that they are at risk of extinction. Adult fish are very rare.

I visited Thailand many times and waited on the banks of the Mekong River for many months. Finally, in May 2008, a group of fishers caught a healthy giant catfish I could tag. As soon as they netted the fish, they gave me a call. I rushed to the river with my team and our equipment. We tagged it quickly and released it back into the river. We were able to follow it as it migrated upstream to spawn.

Over the next few years, we tagged a few other giant catfish—near Hat Khrai and farther south, in Cambodia. But if only we could find more! I worried that they would become extinct in the wild before we could learn any more about them.

Then on November 9, 2015, fishers near the city of Phnom Penh (sounds like PUH-nawm pen) made a very special catch. It was the first and only giant catfish caught that year. It was huge—nearly seven feet (2 m) long, and about 200 pounds (91 kg). When I heard the news, I was thrilled. It seemed like we had waited forever for this. This meant that at least one giant catfish was still alive and well in Cambodia. My crew and I rushed to the spot.

# Saving Giant Catfish

Today, it's against the law to take giant catfish from the river. Nevertheless, a few die accidentally in fishing nets every year. And some people still believe that eating the fish will bring them good luck. But some groups are helping the catfish. Fisheries try to breed giant catfish and release some into the wild. Biologists and groups in several countries are working together to figure out the best places to build dams that won't stop fish from completing their migrations. Together, we can help these fish thrive.

Much to my relief, we got there in time. We were able to tag this rare giant. When it was time to release it, I dived into the water with it. I guided the big catfish down as deep as possible. Ten feet (3 m) below the surface, my ears popped from the great weight of the water above us. It was silent and dark. The muddy waters blocked out the light. I had reached the point where my world ended and the world of the megafish began.

I realized when I released the fish that, in many ways, humans and fish live so differently. Humans live on land, and giant catfish live below, in murky places that humans can't see or visit. I think it's hard for us to appreciate fish because they live in this unseen world. This is a problem for endangered fish like the Mekong giant catfish. We need to know about them in order to appreciate them. And we need to appreciate them in order to protect them. So, my work tagging the fish isn't only about study. It's also about making sure people are aware of these wonderful creatures before it's too late.

On this long river, we know that many types of fish can grow to mega size. As I swam alongside that giant catfish and let it go, I couldn't help but wonder: *Could there be another, even bigger giant hiding right here, deep in the murky waters of the Mekong? And if so, could I find it?*

Zeb Hogan keeps his distance while holding this vampire payara.

# FISH SUPERPOWERS

This red-bellied piranha flashes its teeth as it passes by.

In my search for megafish, I've encountered fish of all sizes. And I've seen many types of fish that have truly amazing powers! While fishing for giants in the Amazon, I was often defeated by a really small fish—the piranha (sounds like per-RON-ah).

Everyone's heard stories of piranhas. These fierce fish live in tropical rivers in South America.

Plenty of fishers there have reeled in a big catch only to find it's been turned into a bare skeleton by a school of hungry piranhas. Piranhas are well known for their super biting powers. They have extremely sharp teeth, and when they spot their prey, they go after it together in a "feeding frenzy."

If you dared to slip into piranha-infested waters, would they swarm you and eat the flesh right off your bones? Piranha behavior looks pretty scary. But in fact, in most places where piranhas live, it's safe to swim in the water. Oddly enough, piranhas seem to have a very good sense of what makes a good meal. And luckily, humans aren't usually on the menu.

Piranhas are somewhat shy fish when they're not in a feeding frenzy. They are

**Did You Know?**

Scientists have found fossils of a *Megapiranha* that lived around 10 million years ago. It was about three feet (1 m) long, and it had a bite as powerful as a lion's.

slow to approach larger animals, unless they sense the animal is in distress. After all, plenty of larger animals eat piranhas. They need to be careful not to get eaten themselves.

Still, people do get bitten from time to time. Most swimmers don't have to worry, though. Piranhas are only found in South America.

Children there know not to swim in areas where fishers clean their fish. The smell of the dead fish sometimes attracts piranhas. It's also important to avoid swimming in isolated pools where piranhas can get trapped. If they've been stuck and haven't been able to find food for a while,

they can become
very aggressive.
I've fished in
the South American
countries of Guyana
(sounds like gahy-AN-uh),
Brazil, and Argentina. In Guyana,
black piranhas are the most common.
They are the largest type of piranha,
growing up to 20 inches (50 cm) long.

The rivers in Argentina are home to
a large, yellow-bellied type. The smaller
red-bellied piranha is the most common in
Brazil. In spite of its smaller size, this type
of piranha is super aggressive!

But wherever I'm fishing, I know almost
immediately if there are piranhas in the
area. No matter what kind of fish I'm

fishing for, as soon as I cast my bait in the water, the piranhas will come for it. Out of all the predatory fish I've studied, they are the quickest to find a piece of bait. Sometimes they'll bite down on it only seconds after it's touched the water.

I've also learned to never put a live piranha in your boat. They live for quite a long time out of water and can still bite. And the piranha's bite is very powerful. It can bend hooks, cut through line, and crush fishing lures. I've even seen fishermen missing parts of their fingers or toes! Believe it or not, the fishermen don't get bitten when they are in the water. But they do get bitten when they forget about a piranha they've caught and put in their boat. Accidentally put your hand or foot

**Did You Know?**

The word "piranha" translates to "tooth fish" in the Brazilian language Tupí.

too close and—
CHOMP!

All piranhas are built to bite. They have incredibly strong jaw muscles. And their jaws are lined with sharp triangle-shape teeth.

When they bite down, they take chunks out of prey, similar to the way you take a bite out of an apple. If you are in South America and you see a big chunk missing from a bait fish or other animal, chances are a piranha was responsible.

Fish mouths come in all shapes and sizes. And you can tell a lot about how a fish eats just by looking at its mouth. One of the weirdest, craziest fish mouths I have ever seen belongs to another South American fish, the payara (sounds like pie-ARE-ah). Even the piranha is no match for these predators. To the payara, a piranha is just a tasty snack!

The payara is sure to be at the top of any list of super biters. For its size, it has some of the longest teeth of any animal on Earth. Two fangs grow from the front of its lower jaw. Some say they look like the teeth of a saber-toothed cat.

Payaras grow to about four feet (1.2 m) long. They can weigh up to 40 pounds (18 kg). And in a full-grown payara, those fangs can be up to six inches (15 cm) long! The oversize fangs are what earned the payara its nickname—the vampire fish. Unlike piranhas, which bite and tear, the payara uses its long fangs to spear prey.

wolffish

## The Wolffish

I've never been bitten by a piranha or a payara. But I have been bitten by another South American fish—the wolffish. It's also locally known as the himara. The largest wolffish grow to about 47 inches (1.2 m) long. They can weigh as much as 88 pounds (40 kg). They are aggressive hunters and super biters!

But while the fangs are impressive, they do only half the work. The payara's mouth is huge. Like a hippopotamus, it can open its mouth incredibly wide.

When it hunts, a payara lies in wait near the bottom of a river. When an unsuspecting fish swims above, the payara opens its mouth and lunges up. The payara snaps its mouth shut with lightning speed. The smaller fish is impaled on the payara's fangs.

Then the payara uses its oversize tongue to get the prey in just the right position in its mouth. And then—GULP! It swallows the fish whole, head first!

There are stories of some payaras eating prey almost half their own size. And fishers have reported seeing the fish with the tail of another fish still sticking out of its mouth!

A pulse from an electric eel can stun or even kill.

# SUPER SHOCKERS

Super biters are amazing, for sure. But did you know that one of the most deadly fish on the planet doesn't have any teeth at all? The electric eel has a special superpower for killing its prey— electricity! These fish have electrical organs that can send out pulses of electricity. Those pulses have enough power to stun, and perhaps even kill, a full-grown man.

I had a chance to fish for electric eels in some of the rivers that feed into the Amazon. And it's one of the scariest fish I've ever encountered!

Electric eel are widespread in South America, and you can never be sure where one will turn up! They live in rivers, lakes, small ponds, streams, and stagnant backwaters. They often hide in underwater caves or among underwater tree branches, roots, or logs. And that's what makes looking for them so scary. No matter where I was, I knew that somewhere in the dark water an electric eel could be hiding. And if I happened to get too close—ZAP!

This is what happened to our cameraman, Colm Whelan (sounds like COMB wee-lan), when we were filming one day. We were wading in waist-deep water. All of a sudden, we saw Colm slump into the water. We rushed to help him. He was stunned and confused. It took us a few seconds to realize what had happened.

Colm had accidentally brushed up against an electric eel. None of us actually saw the eel, but the effects were clear. That shock was strong enough to knock over a full-grown man.

The electric eel may have a classic eel body shape, but it's not really a true eel. It's the largest member of a family of fish called South American knifefish. These fish can grow up to eight feet (2.4 m) long.

The electric eel's jolt is much more powerful than that of any of its smaller knifefish relatives. But all electric fish are able to generate a weak electric field around their bodies. They use their electric field to communicate with each other. They also use it to find their way around or to find food in their dark, murky environment.

An electric eel sends out its super-shocking full-power pulses when it is hunting or when it feels threatened. Most of the time, an eel swims slowly, sending out small pulses of electricity. The pulses bounce, or echo, off objects in its environment. By sensing the echoes, the eel can tell how far away and how big those objects are.

# American Paddlefish

The American paddlefish lives in the Missouri and Mississippi Rivers. This may be one of the weirdest-looking fish in the world. It's famous for its huge spatula-shape snout. Paddlefish don't send out shocks like electric eels. But its snout is lined with detectors that can pick up the electrical signals other animals give off. So paddlefish can use their super-sensitive snouts to find prey as they swim through dark, muddy water.

When the eel detects a fish that's just the right size to eat, it slowly moves toward it. When it gets close enough, it blasts the fish with a pulse of electricity. For the fish, it must be like getting hit with a bolt of lightning! The stunned fish can't even move. The eel opens its mouth quickly, sucks the fish in, and swallows it whole.

My friend Dr. Will Crampton is an electric eel expert. Dr. Will said that a shock from an electrical outlet in your house is 110 volts. That's nothing compared to the shock that an eel can give! Dr. Will said an average eel can produce a shock of more than 700 volts. Some people have said that even large horses have been stunned and killed by eel shocks.

When studying electric eels, our goal was to measure them and find out if bigger eels were stronger shockers than smaller ones. To do that, we were going to have to actually catch some and hold them in our hands.

We were definitely going to need some protective covering. So, we put on funny-looking rubber overalls and gloves. Rubber doesn't conduct electricity. I just hoped it would be thick enough to shield us from the shocks!

In order to find the eels, we used an electricity-detecting device. We waded into the water and dipped the device in wherever we thought eels might be.

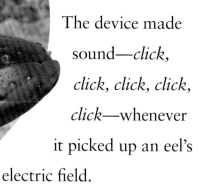

The device made sound—*click, click, click, click, click*—whenever it picked up an eel's electric field.

Once we knew eels were in the area, we set traps for them at night. When we returned the next morning, we discovered we'd caught a few. The smallest was two feet (0.6 m) long, and the largest was more than four feet (1.2 m). They would give us a good comparison of size and power.

Dr. Will had a special voltage detector called an oscilloscope (sounds like uh-SIL-uh-skohp) to measure the eels' power. In some ways, an eel's body is like a big battery. We pressed one of the detector's wires to the smaller eel's head and the other wire to the end of its tail. When the eel pulsed, the device measured the result: 550 volts! About five times stronger than a typical electrical outlet! Could the bigger eel possibly be even more powerful?

We attached the device. The big eel pulsed, and Dr. Will could hardly believe the results. Its shock was 860 volts! That may be the highest voltage anyone has recorded for any animal, anywhere in the world. That's what I call a super shocker!

### Did You Know?

Eels' thick skin normally insulates them from their own attacks, but when wounded, they *can* accidentally shock themselves!

The long-lived longfin eel swims far and wide during its migration.

# Chapter 3

# SUPER SWIMMERS

You've probably learned about many birds and land animals that travel, or migrate, long distances. But most people don't know that some types of fish migrate, too. These are the super swimmers! They travel incredibly long distances. And to get where they're going, they swim through some dramatically different habitats.

Unlike the electric eel, the New Zealand longfin eel is a true eel. It makes one of the most impressive migrations of any animal on the planet. It's New Zealand's biggest and longest-lived freshwater fish. The largest of them reach lengths of seven feet (2 m) and can weigh more than 50 pounds (23 kg).

The longfin eel is born far out in the Pacific Ocean. Almost as soon as they're born, the babies, or larvae (sounds like LAHR-vay), begin a long journey. They drift on ocean currents for more than a thousand miles (1,600 km), finally reaching the freshwater rivers and streams of New Zealand.

Once they get there, the larvae grow and develop into strong swimmers called elvers. They can battle their way up even the steepest waterfalls. So, it's not surprising that they can be found far upstream. Even in fast-moving creeks and in high mountain lakes!

One of the most amazing experiences that I've had with eels was on the South Island of New Zealand, in a beautiful mountain lake called Lake Rotoiti (sounds like row-toe-EE-tee). This lake is famous for its monster-size eels. And I had a chance to go scuba diving with them!

At first I was a little afraid because I'd heard a story of eels chasing divers and biting fishermen. But as soon as I got in the water with them, I knew those stories were exaggerated (sounds like ig-ZAJ-uh-rey-tid).

The eels were more curious than aggressive. They swam all around me. They seemed to be looking and smelling for something to eat. But lucky for me, they didn't view me as food.

I was able to spend almost an hour underwater with them. I was as curious about them as they were about me. But every time I tried to get a hold of one, it slipped right out of my hands.

Have you ever heard the phrase "as slippery as an eel"? It's not because they're devious (sounds like DEE-vee-uhs). It's because they are impossible to hold on to! Their bodies are covered in slimy mucus, which helps them wriggle safely over land when they need to cross from one lake or stream to another. Longfin eels are not just super swimmers, they are super travelers!

And they are super survivors, too. I was amazed to find out that some of the eels in Lake Rotoiti were more than 100 years old!

Longfin eels make their home in freshwater for nearly all of their adult lives. But when they reach the end of their life span, they must swim back to the place where they were born. Imagine: 100-year-old eels making their way out into the open ocean again. Once more, they will take the thousand-mile (1,600-km) journey—this time in reverse. When they reach their birth spot, they'll spawn, or lay their eggs. The old eels will die. And soon a new generation of longfin eels will be born.

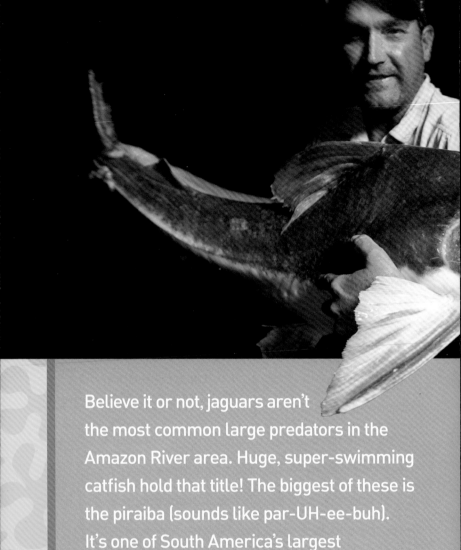

Believe it or not, jaguars aren't
the most common large predators in the
Amazon River area. Huge, super-swimming
catfish hold that title! The biggest of these is
the piraiba (sounds like par-UH-ee-buh).
It's one of South America's largest
freshwater fish. It can grow to more than

**goliath catfish**

eight feet (2.4 m) in length and weigh more than 300 pounds (136 kg). Piraiba make epic migrations up and down the Amazon. During the breeding season, they can swim more than 2,000 miles (3,219 km), from the mouth of the Amazon in Brazil to the river's remote headwaters in Colombia, Ecuador, and Peru.

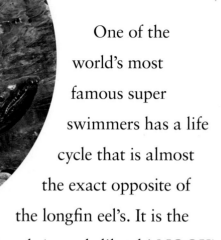

One of the world's most famous super swimmers has a life cycle that is almost the exact opposite of the longfin eel's. It is the Chinook (sounds like shi-NOOK) salmon—the biggest type of Pacific salmon. The largest can grow to almost five feet (1.5 m) in length and weigh more than 100 pounds (45 kg).

Chinook are born in freshwater streams—often far inland or on high mountain slopes. Then they migrate out to the ocean, where they spend their adult lives. At the end of their lives, they migrate back to freshwater to spawn, and then they die. This whole process usually takes only three to seven years. But during that time, the fish may swim all along the Pacific coast of North America.

The rivers of the Pacific Northwest used to run red at certain times of the year. That's because when Chinook salmon are ready to spawn, they turn bright red. Hundreds of them begin to swim upriver at the same time. Often these fish are so large that their backs stick out of the water! These salmon can travel as far inland as Idaho, Montana, and the interior of Alaska.

Sadly, today there aren't nearly as many salmon as there once were. Dams have blocked their migrations in some areas. This has made it difficult for adult fish to reach their spawning grounds.

Many rivers that haven't been dammed, such as the Kenai (sounds like KEE-nye) River on the Kenai Peninsula in Alaska, still have strong salmon runs. The Kenai is famous for its enormous super swimmers. Many of the record-breaking, nearly 100-pound (45-kg) Chinook salmon have been caught there. That's huge, even for the largest of all the Pacific salmon!

White sturgeon (sounds like STUR-juhn) is another giant fish that lives most of its life off the coast of the Pacific Northwest. Like Chinook salmon, they are super swimmers that are born in freshwater but spend most of their lives at sea. Unlike salmon, though, they don't die after they spawn. They make the voyage from ocean to river year after year.

And sturgeon aren't only super swimmers. Like longfin eels, they are also super survivors! White sturgeon have been on Earth for about 100 million years. And individuals have been known to live for more than 100 years.

That means there could be some super swimmers still alive today that were born in the early 1900s. That would be about the same time the Wright brothers were making their historic first flights! But today, even these super survivors are in danger of going extinct because of human activities.

Try to find out all you can about the rivers, streams, and lakes in your local area. The super swimmers that live there need your help and protection!

Zeb Hogan captures and tags a giant stingray.

# IN SEARCH OF GIANT STINGRAYS

Zeb Hogan guides a giant stingray onto a tarp so it can be weighed and measured before being released.

# Chapter 1

# BIGGEST in the WORLD?

**W**hile I was in Thailand tagging giant catfish, I heard tales of huge stingrays. They were living not in the ocean but in the freshwater of the Mekong River. I'd never heard of a stingray in freshwater. But if any of the stories were true, the giant freshwater stingray must be a monster! It would far outweigh even the record-breaking giant catfish.

Some people said they'd seen stingrays that were more than 10 feet (3 m) wide and 20 feet (6 m) long. The stingrays I had seen in the wild were much smaller than that.

I wanted to find one of these legendary giants. But I wasn't sure where to begin looking. Biologists weren't even sure how many might still be alive in the wild.

One of the more interesting stories I had heard was about an older man in the town of Nakorn Sawan (sounds like NA-korn sah-WAN). People said that 15 years ago, this man caught a giant stingray so big that it took a dozen men to haul it out of the water. It barely fit in the back of a huge dump truck. I wondered what it must have been like to come face-to-face with a giant like this.

Did You Know?

Ancient Greek dentists used the venom from the stingray's spine as an anesthetic.

I wanted to talk to the man to find out more.

I knew just where to start: with my friend Dr. Chavalit Vidthayanon (sounds like cha-vah-LET VID-thy-a-non). He's a freshwater fish biologist from Thailand. Sure enough, Dr. Chavalit helped me get in touch with the older man.

As the three of us sat together outside the man's house, the man told me how he had hooked the big stingray. It took him and a partner 11 hours to reel it in! He told me the fish weighed 485 kilograms. That would be more than 1,000 pounds! If this man's story was true, the giant freshwater stingray could be the world's largest freshwater fish.

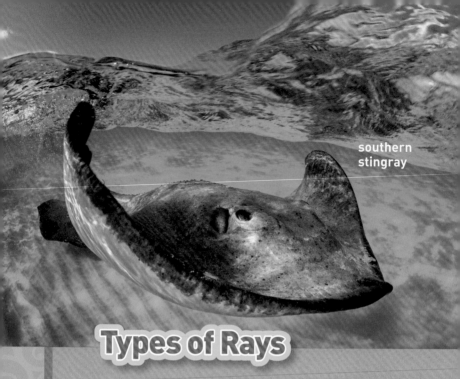

southern stingray

# Types of Rays

When you think of stingrays, you probably think of ocean stingrays. Many types of marine stingrays live in warm coastal areas around the world. Marine stingrays are especially common along the coasts of Southern California and Florida, U.S.A. There are even famous spots named after stingrays, such as Stingray City in the Cayman Islands.

I wanted to believe this man, but I couldn't be sure. In my experience, fishermen love to exaggerate the size of the fish they catch. So unless I see a fish for myself, I'm always a little skeptical (sounds like SKEP-ti-kuhl). It's one thing to hear a story about a huge fish, but it's quite another to see it with my own eyes!

As a scientist, I want to compare people's stories with evidence, measurements, and facts. Without the facts, it's hard to know what's true and what's make-believe. Especially with fish that grow to what sounds like mythical size!

I went back to my work with giant catfish. But the man's story kept running through my mind. I told Dr. Chavalit and others that if anyone caught a giant stingray, I wanted to hear about it. Many months went by with no news. Then, finally, the phone rang.

Someone had caught a stingray that was 14 feet (4.2 m) long! This I had to see! The stingray had been caught in the Mekong River, near the Cambodia-Vietnam border. I rushed there to see it.

Stingrays are close relatives of sharks. Sometimes people call them pancake sharks. That's because they look a little like sharks that have been flattened.

Like sharks, stingrays have skeletons made of cartilage (sounds like KAHR-tuh-lij) rather than bone. But stingrays don't have sharp, pointed teeth like sharks do. Their mouths are on the underside of their bodies. And instead of teeth, they have hard, flat pads that help them crush their prey.

Special sensors in their snouts help them detect their favorites—shrimp, clams, and small fish—even in dark, muddy water.

Stingrays spend most of their time on the river bottom. Their eyes sit on top of their heads, so they can look around while they are hiding in the mud.

Stingrays are not aggressive like some sharks are. But they do have a secret weapon: Attached to the base of their tail is a long stinging spine.

stinging spine

A stingray will only strike if it's frightened or if it feels threatened. But that spine is razor-sharp. And it's coated with venomous mucus. That spine is also strong enough to pierce bone!

I wasn't sure what to expect when I reached the newly captured giant stingray.

Would it really be as big as they said it was? I hoped so, but I didn't want to be disappointed. I tried not to get too excited.

What I saw, however, stunned me. It was by far the biggest stingray I had ever seen in the wild. It wasn't as big as the one the old man said he caught. But seeing this one made me think that even bigger giant stingrays must be out there. No way could this stingray be the only giant in the river! It was time to find out much more about these mysterious monsters!

Scientists have only been studying this fish closely for the past 20 years or so.

There's so much more we want to know.

Yet giant stingrays are disappearing fast. Overfishing, pollution, and loss of habitat have greatly reduced their numbers in some areas. In Thailand, along one river, many stingrays have been reported floating dead after chemical spills.

I hoped that maybe in our search for a record breaker, we would discover the special areas that giant stingrays prefer. I knew we needed to find out all we could about these amazing creatures soon.

We also needed to figure out how to protect them. We needed to figure out where to create protected areas for them to live in before they were all gone. I had finally found one giant freshwater stingray. But how was I going to find others?

Quite a catch! A local man steadies a giant stingray by the tail while Zeb Hogan adjusts the tarp under it.

# Chapter 2

# HIDE-and-SEEK

I traveled up and down the Mekong River in my quest to find giant stingrays. It wasn't easy. These fish live in a murky world that is strange and unfamiliar to us.

I started my search in the local fish markets. I'd visit the markets early in the morning. That's when the vendors would put fresh fish out for sale on trays or large banana leaves.

Most vendors sold catfish or carp, but every once in a while I'd see someone selling stingray. Usually the ray would be cut in pieces, so I couldn't tell how big it was when it was alive. I'd ask the vendors where the fish came from. And they'd tell me the name of a small village along the river.

Traveling by boat, I then visited the small villages where stingrays had been caught. I'd park my boat on the riverbank and walk up to the nearby houses. I'd ask whoever I saw if they knew of anyone who caught stingrays.

In these little towns, everyone knows one another. Everyone knows who farms and who fishes—and especially who fishes for stingray. The stingray fishermen were very talented. Stingrays don't swim into nets, and the everyday rods and reels most fishers use are just not strong enough to land them. Catching stingrays takes special skill and equipment.

After a long search, I finally found one man who knew where and how to catch them. He told me that he liked to fish in shallow sandy areas where stingrays look for food at night.

Instead of fishing line, the man said he used rope, huge hooks, and a 10-pound (4.5-kg) fish as bait. He attached a large rock to the rope to keep the bait on the bottom. Then he tied everything to a floating barrel. He said he left his baited hook in the river overnight. Then he looked for the floating barrel in the morning. Many nights, a stingray would eat all the bait and then try to leave, pulling the rock and barrel behind it all over the river.

I fished with the man for a couple of nights, but we had no luck catching a big one. And I was afraid his way of fishing might exhaust and even hurt the fish if we did catch one. I didn't want that to happen.

At this time, I was searching on a remote stretch of the Mekong, where the villages were small and far apart. I kept asking people if they knew about recent catches. But more often than not, by the time I heard about a catch, the stingray would already have gone to market. I was always too late!

I knew it was time to find another location. Just by luck, I heard about another area where people were catching rays. To my surprise, it was near a major city!

When I got to the city, I joined my friend Rick Humphries and his expert fishing team. If anyone could land a giant, it would be Rick. And I knew that he and his team use special hooks that are not as likely to hurt the fish. They also use heavy-duty gear that helps bring a fish in quickly without exhausting it.

If we did catch a giant, I wanted to be ready to weigh and measure it. So, first I pumped up a large plastic swimming pool and filled it with water from the river. The pool was 10 feet (3 m) wide—big enough to safely hold a giant while we measured it.

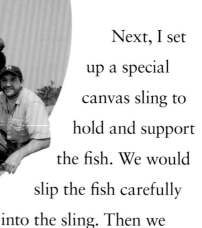

Next, I set up a special canvas sling to hold and support the fish. We would slip the fish carefully into the sling. Then we would hang the sling from a large scale to see how much it weighed. To be sure it was safe, I tested the sling on myself! It was strong enough to weigh me, so I figured it would be sturdy enough for even the biggest fish.

It didn't take long before one of Rick's team members had hooked a big one. Of course, the fish took the bait and then immediately buried itself in the mud on the bottom of the river!

Bringing the fish up was going to take patience and strength. The fisher who caught it said it was like hooking a submarine! No matter how strong you are or how sturdy your gear, it's hard to get such a wide, flat fish out of the mud and up to the surface.

After a lot of effort, we finally had it up near the boat. That's when everyone had to be especially careful. We gently and carefully tied the stingray's stinger flat against its tail with a long strip of cloth. Now the stingray could swing its whiplike tail freely, but we would all be safe. Once its barb was secured, we put the stingray in a soft net, hauled it to shore, then placed it in the pool. This was the first of several we were able to catch, weigh, and measure.

The largest stingray we caught in that area was a female. From snout to tail, she was more than nine and a half feet (3 m) long. She weighed 365 pounds (166 kg). She was a beautiful, healthy fish, but not nearly as big as the monster the old man had described.

As we released her back into the river, we wondered if we'd ever find a larger one in the Mekong. Rick told me he had had some luck getting bigger stingrays in western Thailand, on a wild and remote section of the Maeklong (sounds like MAY-klong) River. We headed there next.

# Short-Tailed River Ray

Believe it or not, there are dozens of species of freshwater stingray! Most of them live in the rivers of South America. In 2015, my team and I went to Argentina to look for the largest of them—the short-tailed river ray.

We explored deep pools, swiftly flowing rapids, shallow sandy banks, and still backwaters. The conditions were brutal! Piranhas often ate our baits. The days were hot and sunny. Sudden storms would drench us. At night, we were eaten alive by mosquitos. After a lot of effort, we finally caught and tagged a 400-pound (181-kg) river ray!

A man comes face-to-face with a giant stingray.

# Chapter 3

# PROTECTING GIANTS

I wanted to be prepared to tag any giants we might be lucky enough to catch in the Maeklong. I planned to use tags that would transmit electronic signals underwater. Each tag held a microchip that would give each fish its own identification number. No one had tried anything like this before. I wanted to make sure we got it right.

The plan was to place underwater receivers six miles (10 km) apart along a stretch of the river. The receivers would record the movements of the tagged fish.

I asked fish veterinarian and stingray expert Dr. Nantarika Chansue (sounds like nahn-tah-REEK-ah CHAN-soo) for help with my plan. We went to the local fish market and bought a small stingray to practice on. The transmitters would have to be inserted under the stingrays' skin. Dr. Nantarika figured out a way to place the transmitters that would not hurt the fish.

Now we were ready to catch a giant! And soon, Rick had one hooked. His fishing pole bent down sharply toward the water's surface as he struggled to bring the fish up. Then suddenly—SNAP! The hook broke, sending Rick tumbling backward. We knew this must have been a huge fish. That hook was made to hold 500 pounds (227 kg)! We were all disappointed to lose that big one.

But soon we had another on the line. This one was a young adult and not as big. Still, it would be great to tag this youngster and be able to observe him as he grew up.

We eased him out of the water and into the pool. Dr. Nantarika placed the transmitter under the stingray's skin near its tail. We were relieved to see that he didn't seem to mind the procedure. We had him back in the river within minutes.

# Giant Whipray

The giant freshwater stingray has a close relative in Australia—the giant whipray. This species was first discovered by scientists in 2008. In 2012, I went to look for them in the remote rivers of northern Australia. During the dry season, these rivers shrink, leaving many isolated, deep pools. In these pools, we found five kinds of predators living side by side— bull sharks, sawfish, saltwater and freshwater crocodiles, and ... whiprays! Could giant whiprays grow even bigger than the giant freshwater stingray? No one knows for sure—not yet, anyway!

We were determined to catch a full-grown adult next. So, Rick and his team got back to work. Later that day, I got a call. Rick said they had a big one on the line. I rushed down to the water to help.

Yes! This was the giant we'd been hoping for. It was almost twice the size of the largest stingray we'd caught in the Mekong. It took 12 men to get it out of the water and into the pool.

Right away, Dr. Nantarika knew the fish was a female. And, even better, she was pregnant! Using a portable ultrasound machine, Dr. Nantarika could see three babies inside. This was incredible news! It meant that there was a healthy breeding population of giant stingrays in this area.

We successfully placed the transmitter under the stingray's skin. I estimated that this fish must weigh more than 600 pounds (272 kg). I had to guess because the crane we needed to set up our scale was late arriving. We couldn't risk keeping the stingray out of the river any longer while we waited. We eased her back into the water and watched as she swam back down into the murky depths.

Two months after we successfully tagged these fish, I went back to the Maeklong. I pulled the first receiver from the water and connected it to my laptop.

Once the data was downloaded, we could clearly see which rays had passed this spot and how many times they had done so. With this data and the data from the other receivers, we could begin to figure out the stingrays' movements.

Tagging has helped us figure out how many stingrays there may be in an area, how far they migrate, and which habitats these giants prefer. Tagging rays has also helped us understand how big and how fast giant stingrays grow.

Every time we catch a ray for the first time, we record the fish's weight and size. If and when that same fish is caught again, we can learn how much it has grown in the time since it was last caught.

All this information will help people develop better laws that will allow local fishers to get food from the rivers, while at the same time giving fish the time and space they need to breed, grow, and thrive.

Most of all, this information will help people decide on the best places to create protected areas for giant stingrays.

While I was processing some of our new data, I spotted an interesting news story. It described a 617-pound (280-kg) stingray caught in central Thailand. A local fisher caught it in an urban area. Most people living in the city near the river had no idea fish this big existed!

Could the world's largest freshwater fish live just yards from the multistoried apartment buildings of a large, modern city? I now believe that the old man's story, and other stories about supergiant 1,000-pound (454-kg) stingrays, could indeed be true. So, I will keep on searching!

### THE END

# DON'T MISS!

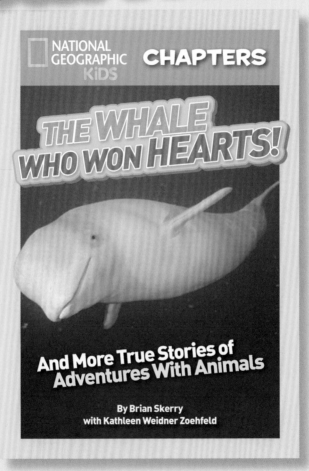

NATIONAL GEOGRAPHIC KiDS **CHAPTERS**

## THE WHALE WHO WON HEARTS!

And More True Stories of Adventures With Animals

By Brian Skerry
with Kathleen Weidner Zoehfeld

**Turn the page
for a sneak preview . . .**

Gray reef sharks swim over the corals around the Line Islands in the Pacific Ocean.

# THE REEF
## Where
## SHARKS RULE

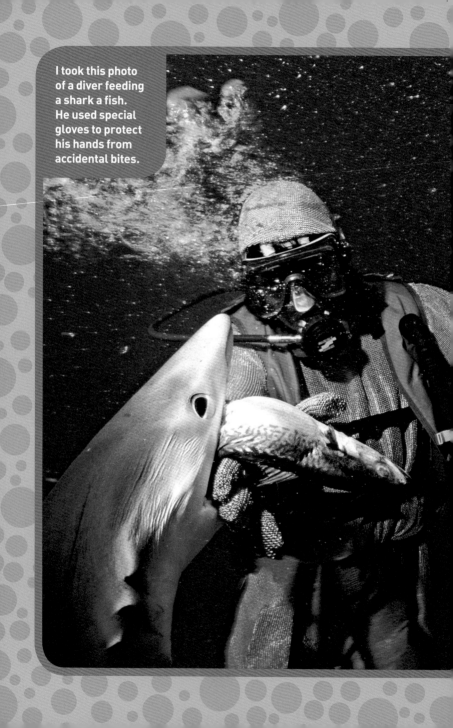

I took this photo of a diver feeding a shark a fish. He used special gloves to protect his hands from accidental bites.

# Chapter 1

# HOOKED ON SHARKS

'll never forget the first time I swam with a shark. It was almost 30 years ago. At that time, most people thought of sharks as sharp-toothed killing machines. The last thing any diver wanted was to run into a shark! But I had a chance to help a group of scientists. They were studying sharks off the coast of Rhode Island. Even though I was a little afraid, I joined them.

I thought it would be interesting to get to know these animals better.

We sailed 20 miles (32 km) offshore. The scientists put out some bait. A five-foot (1.5-m)-long blue shark swam up to check it out. I was in the water taking photos. For more than an hour, I drifted in the chilly water. The shark swam right beside me. But it never tried to attack. It just seemed curious. And I was curious about the shark. All my fears melted away. I stared at it in total awe. The shark had a slender body. It had long, winglike fins. It looked like a finely designed aircraft.

Ever since that day, I've been hooked on sharks. I've swum with blue sharks many times since then. I've swum with other kinds, too. Thanks to scientists and explorers, people have begun to better understand sharks. They're no longer seen as monsters. Like lions in the grasslands of Africa, sharks are the top predators in their ocean homes. Predators are animals that hunt other animals for food. But sharks never hunt humans on purpose.

It can be scary to hear about a shark biting a surfer at the beach. But such attacks are very, very rare. A shark may strike if a human threatens it. Or it may mistake a human for a seal or other natural prey. But humans are a greater danger to sharks than they are to us.

## Did You Know?

Whenever a shark loses a tooth, a new one comes in to replace it. A shark can grow thousands of teeth in its lifetime.

# The Scoop on Sharks

Sharks first swam the seas around 400 million years ago. That's almost 200 million years before the first dinosaur walked on Earth. A shark's skeleton is not bony. It's made up mostly of cartilage (sounds like CAR-tuh-lij). Your ears and the tip of your nose are also made of cartilage. Today, there are more than 400 types of shark. The smallest is the dwarf lantern shark. It's smaller than a human hand. The biggest shark is the whale shark (above). It's as long as a school bus!

People kill more than 100 million sharks each year. Most are taken for their fins, which are used in shark fin soup.

Way too often, I see badly hurt sharks. I see some tangled in long fish lines. I see others caught in pieces of plastic trash.

Over the years, I've found it harder and harder to find sharks anywhere. Because of overfishing and pollution, the oceans' great predators are in danger of dying out completely.

Not long ago, I was asked to join a National Geographic expedition (sounds like eks-puh-DISH-un). The members of the expedition were headed to one of the most remote, or faraway, places on the . . .

**Want to know what happens next? Be sure to check out *The Whale Who Won Hearts!* Available wherever books and ebooks are sold.**

# INDEX

**Boldface** indicates illustrations.

American paddlefish 53, **53**

Biodiversity 15
Blue sharks 106

Cartilage 78, 108
Chinook salmon **66,** 66–68

Electric eels **48,** 49–52, **51,**
54–57, **56**

Giant barbs 35
Giant dog-eating catfish 35
Giant freshwater stingrays
catching 85–90, 94–95
protected areas 81, 100
pups 87
tagging **70–71,** 93–95, 98–99
weighing and measuring
87–88, **88,** 89–90
Giant whiprays 96, **96**
Goliath catfish **64–65**
Gray reef sharks **102–103**

Map 4–5
*Megapiranha* 41
Mekong giant catfish
captured **6–7, 8, 26**
eggs 14, 24
growing awareness 22
helping to save 25, 33
migration 24, 29, 31
tagging 29–32, 34, 35

New Zealand longfin eels
**58,** 60–63

Overfishing 29, 81, 109

Payaras **36–37,** 44–45, 47
Piraiba 64–65
Piranhas **38,** 39–45, **42,** 91
Pollution 29, 81, 109

Red-bellied piranhas **38,** 42
Redtail catfish 11

Sharks 78, **102–104,**
105–109, **108**
Short-tailed river rays
91, **91**
South American knifefish
51–52
Southern stingray **76**
Stingrays
cartilage 78
number of species 94
special sensors 79
stinging spine 75, 79, **79**
types of 76

Vampire payara **36–37**
Venom 75

Whale sharks 19, 108, **108**
White sturgeon 68–69
Wolffish 46, **46**

# MORE INFORMATION

channel.nationalgeographic
.com/wild/monster-fish

Learn more about the fish
featured in this book and Zeb
Hogan's other adventures
around the world. Check out
articles, facts, and exclusive
digital extras from Nat Geo
WILD's *Monster Fish.*

environment.national
geographic.com/environment/
freshwater/mekong-giant
-catfish

National Geographic's profile of
the Mekong giant catfish

environment.national
geographic.com/environment/
freshwater/giant-freshwater
-stingray

National Geographic's profile of
the giant freshwater stingray

Additional educator resources:

nationalgeographic.org/media/
giant-catfish

Video with accompanying
interviews, resources, and
vocabulary about Zeb's work to
save the Mekong giant catfish.

# ACKNOWLEDGMENTS

Thanks to the book team, Brenna Maloney, Shelby Alinsky, Kathryn Williams, Jeff Heimsath, Ruth Ann Thompson, and Sanjida Rashid.

# CREDITS

Cover, Erin Buxton/National Geographic Channel; Back Cover, Rebecca Hale/National Geographic Creative; 6-7, Zeb Hogan; 8, Zeb Hogan; 15, jakkreethampitakkull/Getty Images; 16, Zeb Hogan/National Geographic Channel; 22 (UP), Zeb Hogan; 22 (LO), Zeb Hogan; 25, Roland Seitre/Nature Picture Library; 26, Zeb Hogan; 29, Zeb Hogan; 33, Zeb Hogan/National Geographic Creative; 36-37, Paulo Velozo/National Geographic Channel; 38, Mark Bowler/Getty Images; 42, Jelger Herder/Buiten-beeld/Minden Pictures; 46, Paulo Velozo/National Geographic Channel; 48, WaterFrame/Alamy; 51, Erin Buxton/National Geographic Channel; 53, Michael Forsberg/National Geographic Creative; 56, Norbert Wu/Minden Pictures; 58, Tobias Bernhard/Getty Images; 64-65, Erin Buxton/National Geographic Channel; 66, Michael Quinton/Minden Pictures; 70-71, Zeb Hogan; 72, Zeb Hogan; 76, Alex Mustard/Minden Pictures; 79, Rob Taylor/National Geographic Channel; 80, Singha Quansuwan/National Geographic Channel; 82, Zeb Hogan; 88, Zeb Hogan; 91, Paulo Velozo/National Geographic Channel; 92, Zeb Hogan; 96, Zeb Hogan; 111, Paulo Velozo/National Geographic Channel; 112, National Geographic Channel